Baseball Talk

By Malcolm Wells

What Do They Really Mean By That, Anyway?

WILLOW CREEK PRESS

MINOCQUA, WISCONSIN

Published in 1997 by Willow Creek Press
P.O. Box 147, Minocqua, Wisconsin 54548

For information on other Willow Creek titles,
call 1-800-850-WILD

ISBN 1-57223-082-7

Printed in the U.S.A.

Special thanks to John Kuenster, editor of *Baseball Digest,* for publishing
many of these cartoons. Six of them also appeared in *The Cape Codder.*
Captain Bill Froelich did more than anyone to push me into completing
and publishing the cartoons. And I was delighted when both Joe
Castiglione and Bob Starr said kind things about them during Red
Sox radio broadcasts.

—M.W.

He stands deep in the batter's box.

Mrs. Lowe.

Mrs. Lowe outside.

Mrs. Lowe outside for a ball.

Down too low for a ball.

Mrs. Lowe inside.

Mrs. Lowe inside for a ball.

He throws the ball and Mrs. Lowe, and the count is full again with a man on base.

Owen Thieu is the count.

Now the count is full.

A two-ball count.

The count gets ahead of him.

Manny has a two-two count on him.

Chuck chokes up a bit as the two-two count gets full.

The count goes deep.

He has the power to go deep.

He takes him deep.

Let's see what he comes up with now.

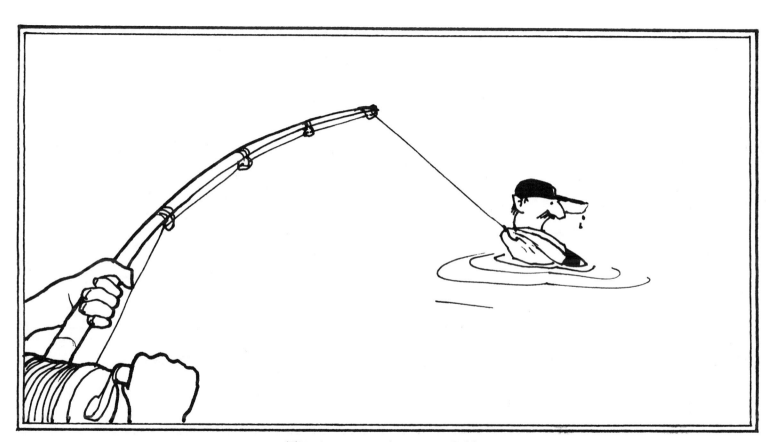

This brings up the center fielder.

That brings up the catcher.

He reached the deepest part of the park.

They tried to bring one in by the back door.

He takes a slider in there.

Kenny goes outside with a slider.

He looks at a slider, down and out.

A slider caught him looking on the outside corner.

The pitching coach pays a visit to the mound.

He gets a visit from the bench.

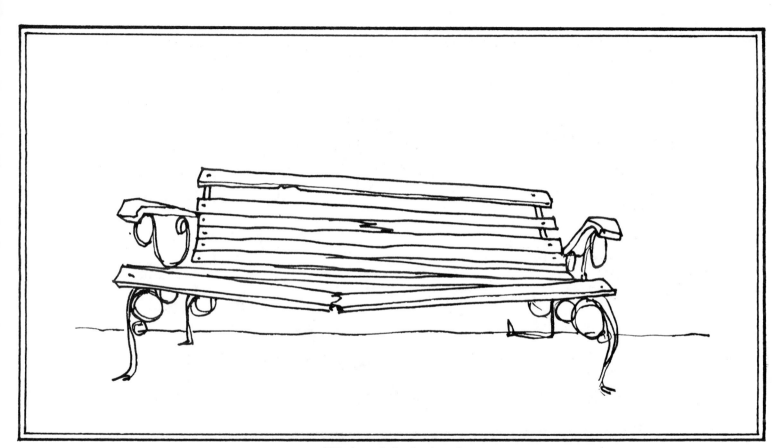

His bench is depleted.

Ike deals inside and high.

Todd puts a little something on the ball this time.

Jerry was touched in the first for a hit.

Now he comes to the plate with a sinking ball.

Angelo paints the outside corner.

Frank runs inside for a ball.

Kelly sets at the belt, delivers.

Chris would love to get a double-play ball off this guy.

Johnny winds and delivers.

Big Ted delivers, and the lead-off hitter takes it.

Foxx goes downstairs for a ball.

He fanned two batters.

Suggested by John Kuenster

He kicks and delivers.

He came in with his heater that time.

Suggested by Bill Sweatt

He's having trouble finding the plate.

He touches the bill on his cap.

Suggested by John Kuenster

Here's the two-two pitch.

He froze him with a curve.

Suggested by John Kuenster

He might go inside with a right-handed hitter.

Quickly he gets ahead of the hitter.

He has excellent breaking stuff.

He took a little something off it that time.

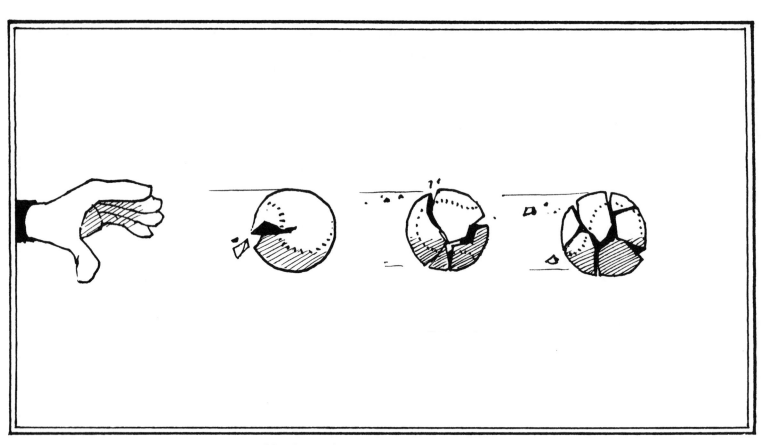

He threw three straight breaking balls.

The fast ball is in there.

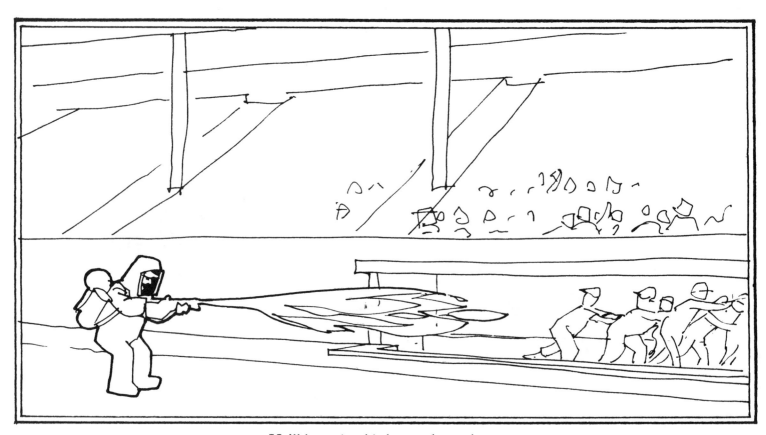

He'll be trying his best to burn them.

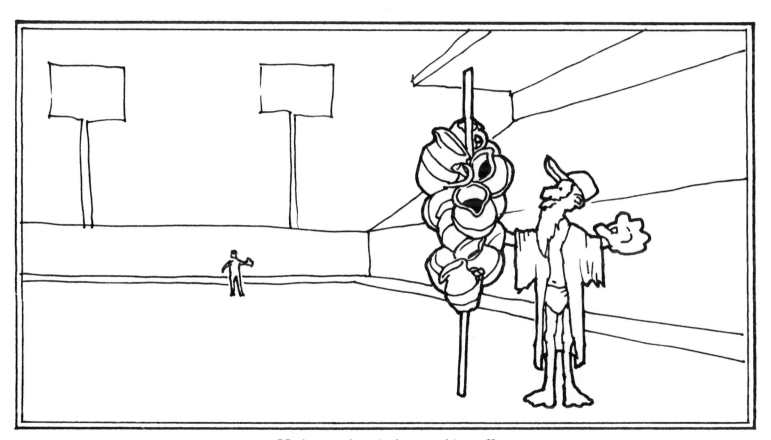

He has twelve pitchers on his staff.

He works him up and in.

He shakes off a sign.

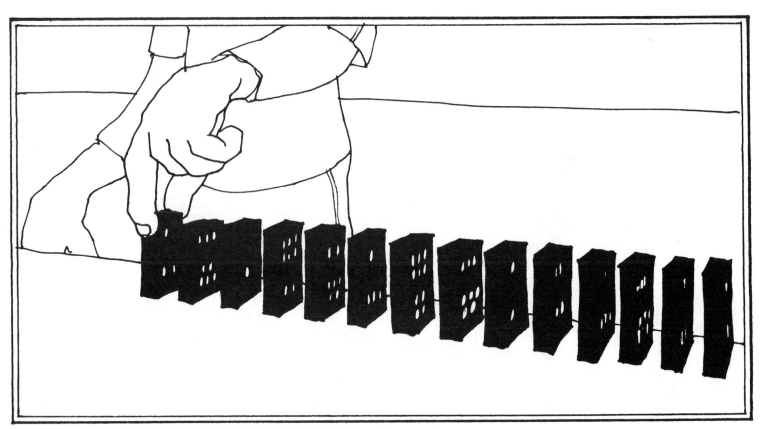

He has set down fourteen in a row.

In the bullpen, Adams is getting up.

He begins to loosen in the bullpen.

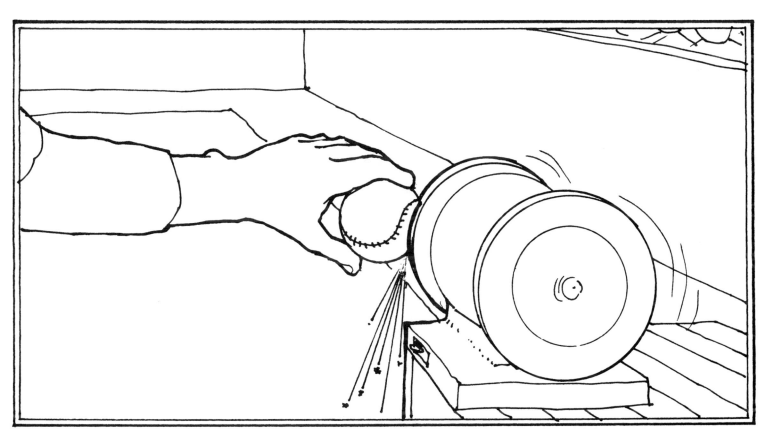

A sharp ground ball.

The veteran left-hander.

He goes to the belt.

There's a pitch outside.

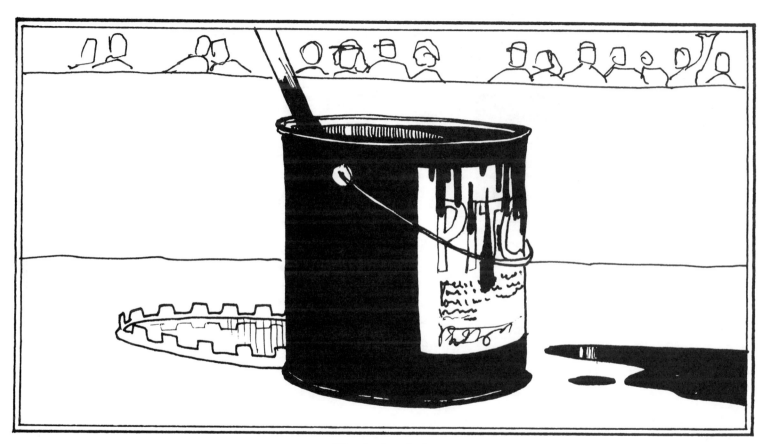

Here's the pitch.

Pitchout.

Wild pitch.

John draws a walk.

Louis takes a ball from him.

Stevie waits as the pitcher winds.

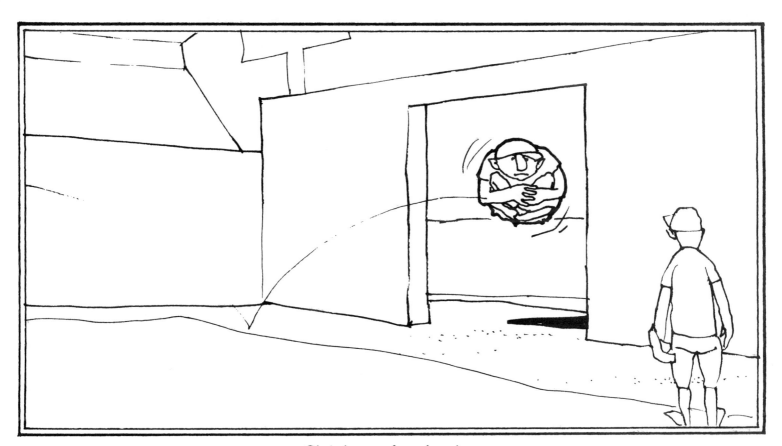

Chris bounced out last time.

Carter takes Lincoln off the wall.

It's two and one on the hitter.

He'll face the reliever with a man on base.

He pulled the ball to right.

Suggested by John Kuenster

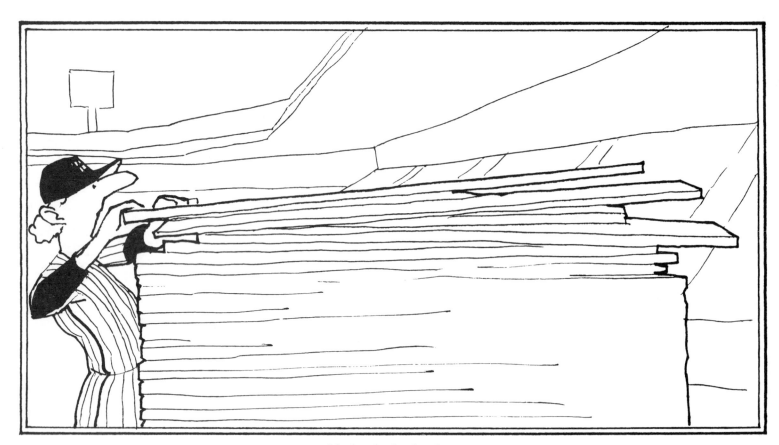

He levels the lumber.

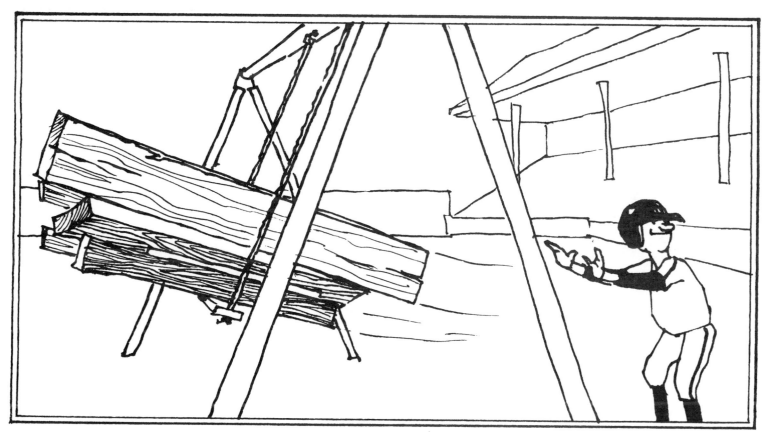

He swings some heavy lumber.

Suggested by John Kuenster

He went down and got it and drilled it.

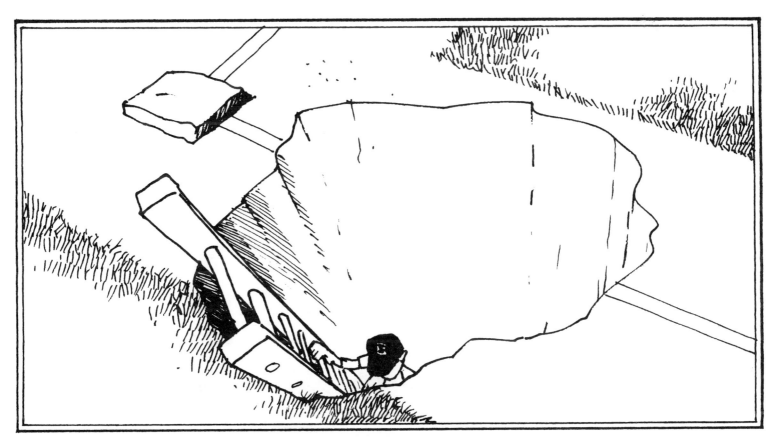

He went down and got a piece of it and lined it.

He's the cleanup hitter.

Suggested by John Kuenster

He hits one upstairs.

That one handcuffed him.

Suggested by John Kuenster

He chokes up a little.

He looks at a slow breaking ball.

He hit that one downtown.

Suggested by John Kuenster

He doubled tonight going the opposite way.

He drags a bunt toward first.

Suggested by John Kuenster

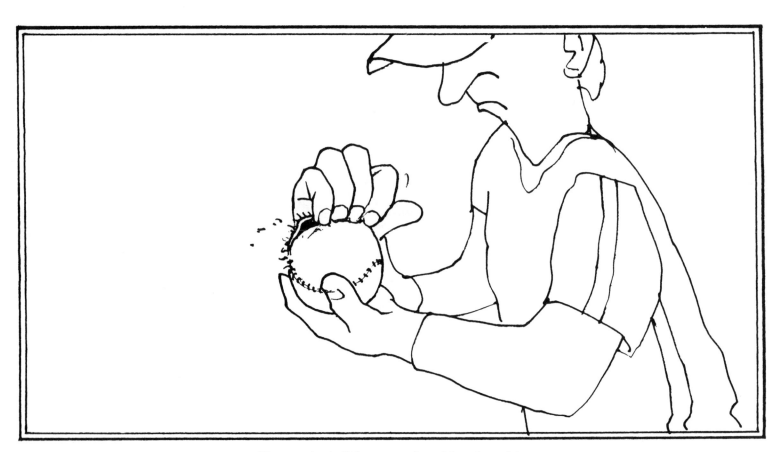

He got the ball he wanted and he ripped it.

He got a piece of a breaking ball.

Switch hitter.

He hits a soft liner.

He's still searching for his first home run.

A swing and a miss.

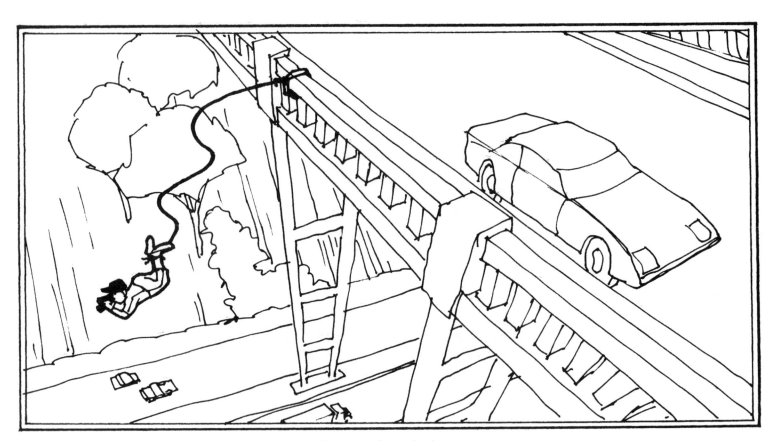

He went down looking.

He has a little hitting streak going.

He went down swinging.

He drove in a run.

A pinch hitter.

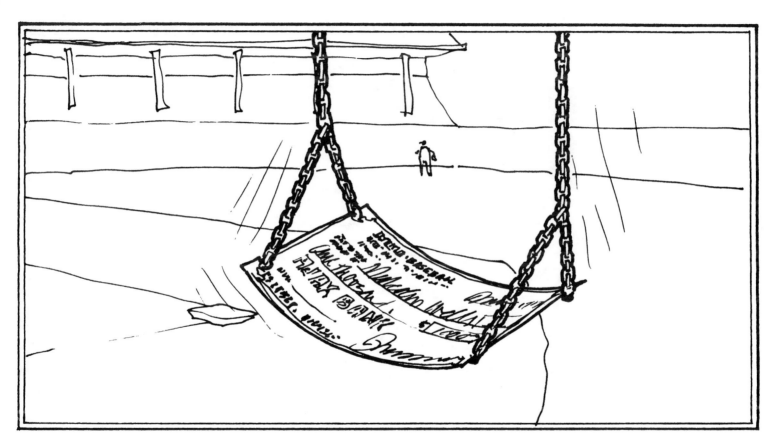

Check swing.

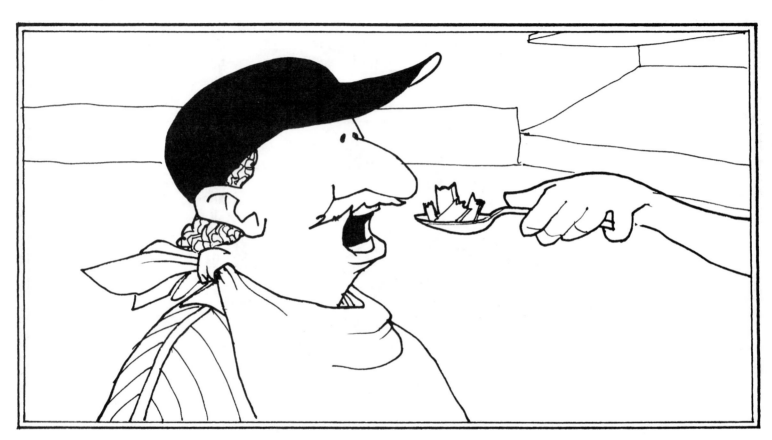

They fed him nothing but breaking stuff.

A called strike at the knees.

He stays away from an upstairs fast ball.

He has a little pop in his bat.

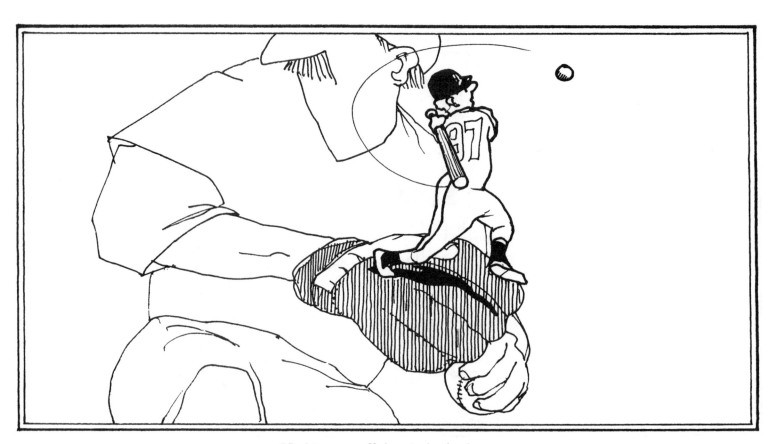

He hits one off the pitcher's glove.

He hammered it over the right field fence.

He looks at a strike.

He ripped a fast ball off the scoreboard.

Joey rips one up the middle.

He ripped a solid single off the wall.

He waits for the delivery.

He hits it toward the hole.

He's a dead fast ball hitter.

Passed ball.

Greg has the sign and delivers.

Hartley again flashes the sign.

Joe gets the sign from the catcher.

Looking in to get the sign.

Harding can swing a mean bat.

Tommy chokes on the bat.

Hank is struggling a bit with the bat.

Brownie's been swinging the bat well of late.

He hit it off the end of the bat.

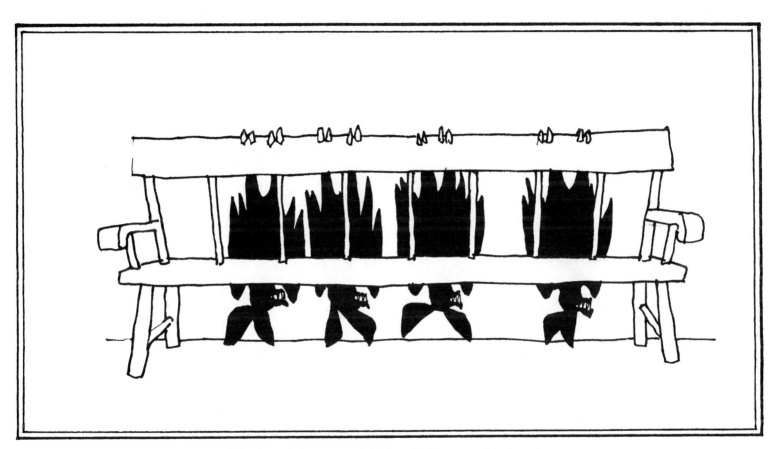

He doesn't have any left-handed bats on his bench.

He looks as if he doesn't want to be up there with a bat in his hand.

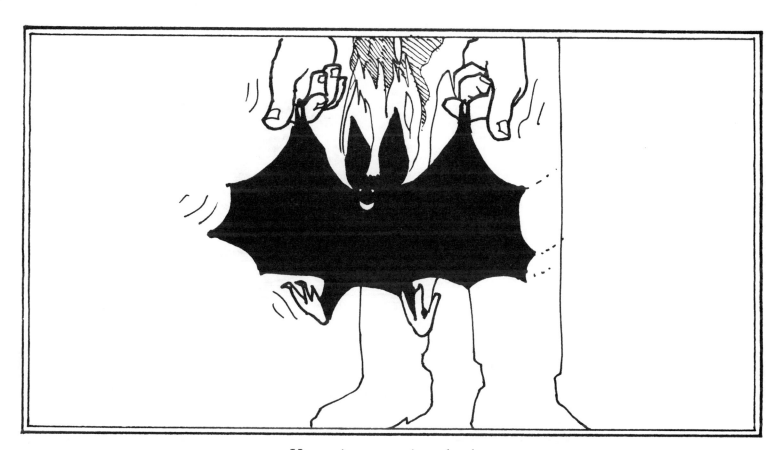

He continues to swing a hot bat.

Eddie gets back behind the plate.

A base hit.

A stolen base.

He has stolen 41 bases.

The bases are loaded.

The bases are loaded.

They leave them loaded.

A base on balls.

He comes home on Billy's fly.

Jack hits a fly.

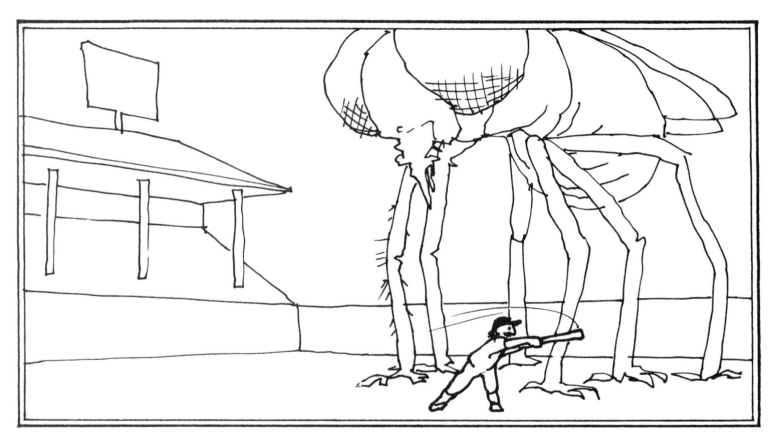

He hits a towering fly.

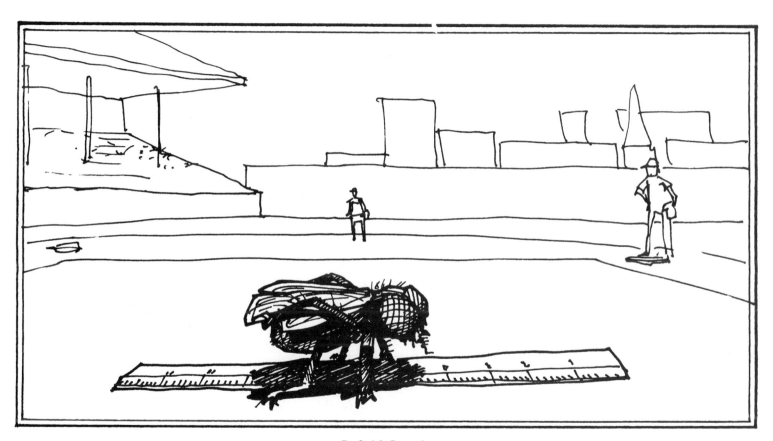

Infield fly rule.

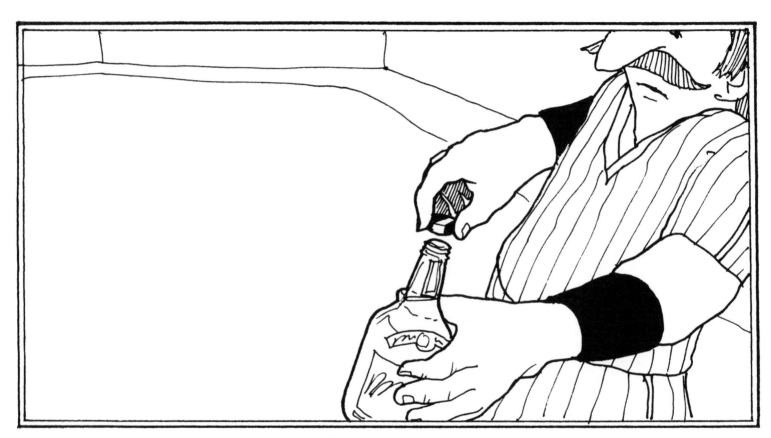

Willy opens the fifth.

He hit his fifth today.

The bottom of the fifth.

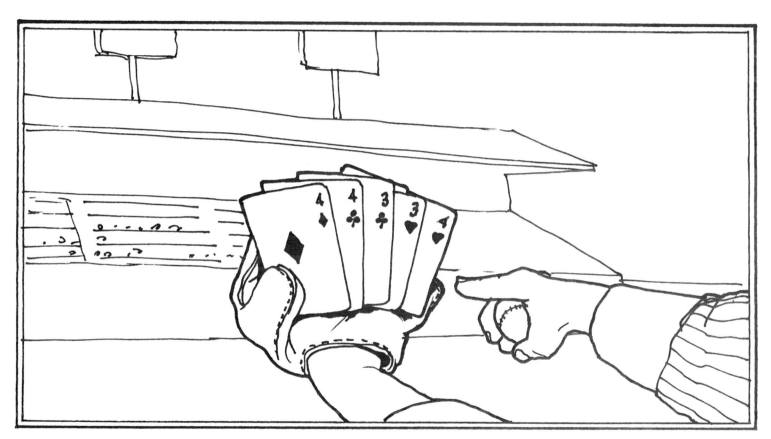

A full house here tonight.

The ball park is full.

They play Strauss the other way.

Butch tries to get a piece of it.

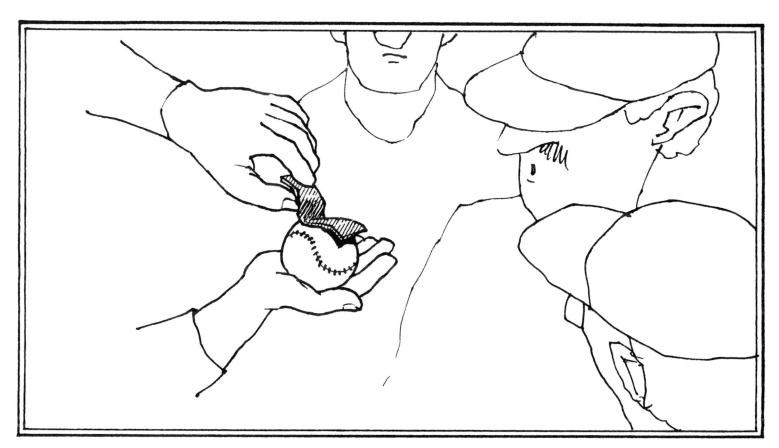

Nick tries to put some leather on the ball.

Let's see if the hit-and-run is on.

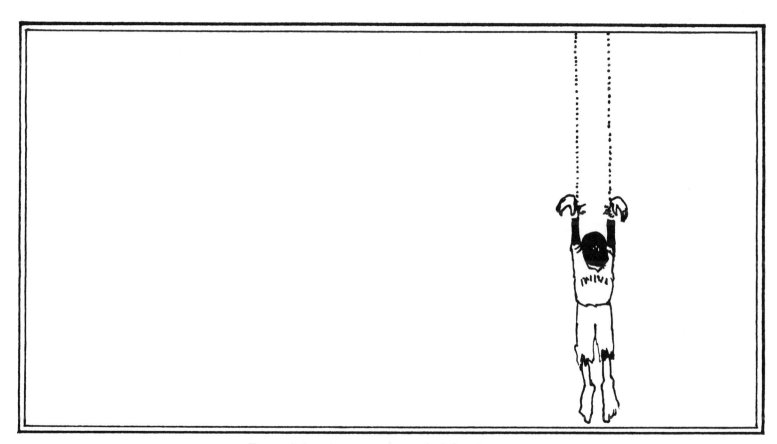

Danny's brother was suspended for the season.

And now the league-leading hitter is on deck.

A high chopper over the mound

Suggested by Elizabeth Lindsay

That was a bang-bang play, folks.

Suggested by Bill Sweatt

Kelly's camped at second.

He's put up some big numbers this year.

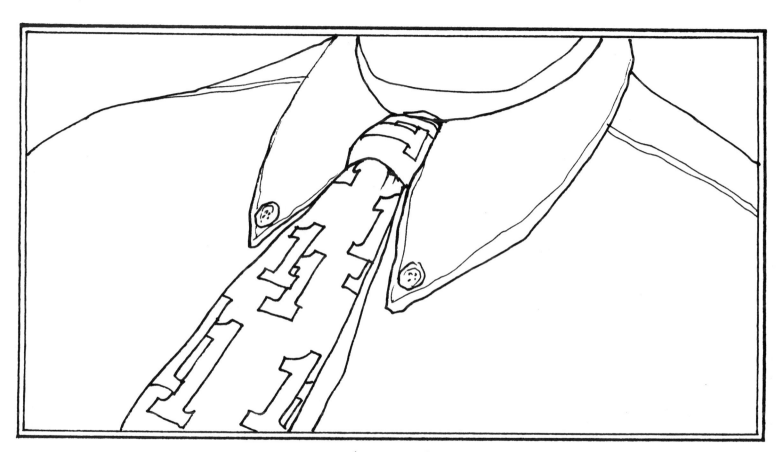

A one-one tie.

They break the one-one tie.

The squeeze play is on.

He looks at one right down the middle.

The youngster took one into the net.

A run home.

They're looking for the long ball.

He's a hard man to double up.

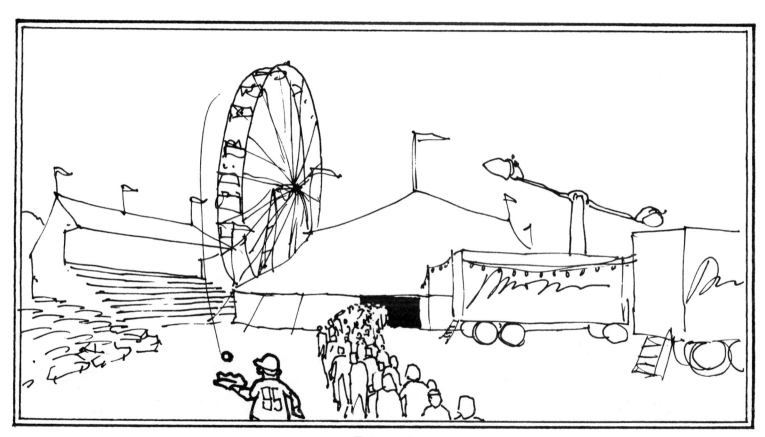

Fair catch.

Tonight's line-up.

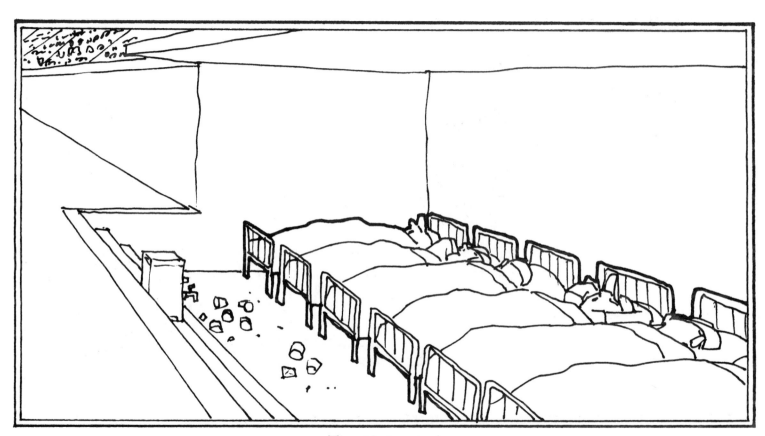

The side is retired.

They were retired in order.

The Red Sox eight–two over the Jays.

He was caught stealing.

He's just up from the minors.

He goes back onto the track.

Foul line.

A ground ball toward the hole.

A shoestring catch.

He drifts to his left.

He has a short lead.

Playing under the lights.

Double play.

They've stranded four.

He's been ejected.

Fielder's choice.

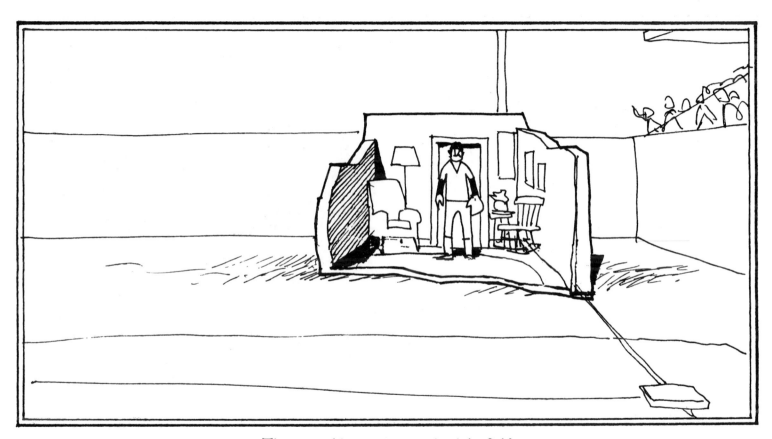

They gave him some room in right field.

Two men are out.

The infield is drawn in.

In the clubhouse.

Back-to-back walks.

A double-header.

He checks the runner.

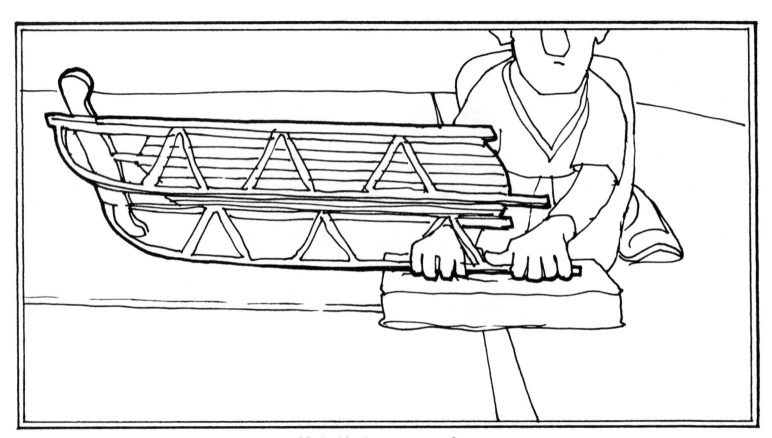

He holds the runner on first.

Suicide squeeze.

Moe puts it away near the coach's box.

He steps out of the box.

He gets back in there.